ISBN (Paperback Edition): 978-1-7337208-0-9
ISBN (eBook Edition):   978-1-7337208-1-6
ISBN (Hardback Edition): 978-1-7337208-2-3

Printed and bound by IngramSpark in the United States of America

First Printing February 2019

Book Editing by Robin L. Flanigan, TheKineticPen.com
Book cover design and formatting by Nelly Murariu, PixBeeDesign.com

Visit SurpriseDateChallenge.com

Be the Happiest Couple You Know

The
SURPRISE
DATE
CHALLENGE

DANA LAM & MARTIN KUPPER

Remember the passion you felt
for your partner in the beginning
of your relationship?

You couldn't wait to see each other,
to hear the sound of each other's
voice. You were spontaneous, and
may even have swapped gifts for
no reason at all.

Does all that sound

as if it belongs in a

land far, far away?

∞

"Desire makes life happen. Makes it matter. Makes everything worth it. Desire is life. Hunger to see the next sunrise or sunset, to touch the one you love, to try again."

— *Karen Marie Moning*

Contents

11 Introduction

15 Why Dating Your Partner Is Important

23 Let's Get Started!

31 Twelve Months of Surprise Dates

 33 January: Vision Board

 37 February: Scavenger Hunt

 41 March: Romantic Tent

 45 April: Art Night

 49 May: Spa Day

 53 June: Mini Road Trip

 57 July: Salsa Dancing

 61 August: DIY Project

 65 September: Cooking Class

 69 October: Volunteering

 71 November: Tropical Island

 73 December: Gingerbread House

77 Being the Happiest Couple You Know

81 Proclamation

> **"** Happily ever after
> is not a fairy tale
> — it's a choice. **"**
>
> — *Fawn Weaver*

Introduction

Most of us yearn for the fairy tale romance—we want to meet our soulmate and live happily ever after.

Unfortunately, as we know from divorce statistics, the number of couples we see settling in their relationships, and our own unsatisfying experiences in love, the fairy tale rarely—if ever—comes true.

That doesn't have to be the case.

We've created a formula for couples who want to make the leap from falling in love to sustaining a fulfilling long-term relationship—and being the happiest couple they know.

The secret ingredient is in the Surprise Date Challenge. Rooted in mystery and adventure, the surprise dates are planned by each partner every month. The challenge is for each of you to do the planning for a three-month stretch.

We know it may be hard to believe that something so simple can make a significant impact in your relationship. But trust us—and the couples you'll meet on these pages. Our recipe, along with the interactive ingredients sprinkled throughout the book, will make your relationship better than you've ever imagined.

You truly can have everything you desire in your relationship, and it all begins with the Surprise Date Challenge.

Here's to your happily ever after.

Dana and Marty

> "If you live to be 100, I hope to live to be 100 minus one day, so I never have to live without you."
>
> — *Winnie-the-Pooh*

Why Dating Your Partner Is Important

The couples we meet are usually upfront about putting their relationship on the back burner, able to give each other only the scraps of what's left after a busy day. Add children to the mix, on top of work demands—exhausting!—and they're even more hard-pressed to spend quality time together.

No wonder a night out on the town can sound like a chore.

But date nights are essential no matter how long you've been together. Just because relationship studies have shown that romantic love dwindles over time—yes, the initial butterflies disappear—doesn't mean you have to swap passion for boredom.

Date nights don't have to be extravagant or expensive.
(In fact, they cost a lot less than a divorce.)

Our motto:

Have fun!

Did you know that novelty in a relationship—trying new things—can create the chemical surges of courtship?

That's what a State University of New York at Stony Brook study found. After ten weeks, couples who did not go on any dates, and couples who spent time together only once a week doing familiar activities, such as going to dinner and a movie, reported little or no change in the satisfaction of their relationship. Couples who participated in exciting, adventurous activities for the first time, however, reported notable increases in their level of satisfaction.

As Dr. Sue Johnson points out in her seminal book
Hold Me Tight: Seven Conversations for a Lifetime of Love:

> "Everything moves and changes, but
> for love relationships there is no 'way it is'
> anymore. We are finally learning how to
> 'make' and 'keep' love alive."

Don't succumb to the long-held belief that relationships inevitably become stale over time. There's too much at stake. Instead, keep in mind the power of enjoying new experiences together—and plan to make them happen. It will be one of the best investments you'll ever make.

Dana didn't know about the importance of novelty when she was married, and ultimately that played a role in the disintegration of her marriage. She shares the following story to convey the heart-wrenching challenges we know so many of you face—challenges that may be avoided with some creativity and a mutual commitment to keep things fresh and exciting.

I remember when I met Henry for the first time, at work. I didn't give him much thought at first, but over the next seven months we became friends. A romance developed and we were suddenly on the fast track down the aisle. I believed our marriage would last a lifetime, and that divorce was not an option, especially once we had children.

We started a family immediately.

The first few years flew by, with most of our time spent attending to our sons, Ethan and Harrison.

We had regular date nights, but they were the usual dinner and a movie. I'm not sure exactly when it happened, but one night I went to sleep with my lover and woke up next to my roommate.

The thought of ripping our family apart made me sick to my stomach. Even so, I couldn't fathom staying in a loveless relationship that existed for the sake of the kids.

I vividly remember the first night I moved from our big house to a 450-square-foot studio to figure things out.

I had never felt so alone. Strange noises—and my thoughts—made it hard to fall asleep.

All of a sudden I could relate to a divorced friend, who had called months before to say how sad and alone she felt because her son had left to spend the weekend with his dad. At the time I was a little envious, frankly. I'd told her how lucky she was, and that if I had the house to myself I'd take baths, drink wine, and read.

I wanted none of that. I cried myself to sleep, wondering if I had made the right decision.

I did make the right decision, but I truly believe that if Henry and I had put our relationship first we would still be together. Our family would still be together.

While I can't change the past, I now have a sensational partner who had the brilliance to come up with the Surprise Date Challenge. It has made our relationship exceptionally fulfilling.

And we're dedicated to a lifetime of adventure!

With hope and happiness,

Dana

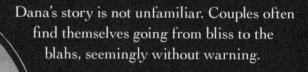

Dana's story is not unfamiliar. Couples often find themselves going from bliss to the blahs, seemingly without warning.

When I came up with the idea for the Surprise Date Challenge, it was in the spirit of spending time with Dana in unconventional ways. I remembered how I typically felt at the beginning of a relationship— the butterflies, the endless hours on the phone, the anticipation of seeing each other again—and I wanted those feelings to last. I wanted to find a way to bottle them up, to create a secret elixir to indulge in again and again.

The truth is, I had no choice but to do something different. My standard playbook of dates, with simple variations, was simply not going to work with Dana. She's remarkably creative, and for the first time I felt compelled to step up my game.

Interestingly enough, one of the surprise dates that had the deepest impact was one of the simplest and most inexpensive. I sent Dana an invitation to dinner, with instructions to meet me at our house at 4:30 p.m. I told her to wear her favorite green top, black leggings, black boots, and a black wig she'd bought the previous year for Halloween. All day, she later told

me, she was enthusiastically curious about where we'd be going.
We wound up at a Fat Tuesday Mardi Gras party at a restaurant.
An otherwise simple dinner had a great twist—and that's what
made it an adventure.

Years later, the power of date nights in general—and surprise dates
in particular—has dramatically improved our relationship in a
number of key areas.

Our communication has elevated our conversations, so that we
listen first and respond without judgment or criticism. Our desire
and passion continues to grow not only for each other, but for our
individual pursuits. Our commitment to make our relationship
a priority has made us exponentially happier as individuals, as
well as a couple. And the results we've witnessed firsthand, in
deepening our love for each other, has decreased our stress levels.

Because of our allegiance to regular date nights—these
seemingly small deposits that do wonders for our
Love Bank Account—I have an obligation
to think about what makes Dana light up,
what she might find exhilarating.

That alone keeps the thrill alive for me.

Here's to making love last,

Marty

" We are all a little
weird and life's a little
weird, and when we
find someone whose
weirdness is compatible with
ours, we join up with them and
fall in mutual weirdness and call
it love. "

— Robert Fulghum
(Dr. Seuss)

Let's Get Started!

The key to becoming the happiest couple you know lies in taking one simple step at a time. Here are the first five to help the surprise date planner move from intention to action:

STEP 1	Find an idea for the date you want to plan.
STEP 2	Choose a specific time for the date, make sure your partner is available, and put it on the calendar.
STEP 3	Secure plans by making reservations, purchasing tickets, etc.
STEP 4	No later than four hours before the date, communicate the dress code and any other relevant information to your partner.
STEP 5	Show up ready to have a great time!

If you think your partner may be uninterested in participating, you're not alone. We hear this concern all the time.

Turns out, more often than not, a seemingly uninterested partner is very interested—just maybe not all that good at planning. As a result, you may have become the primary date planner purely by default.

Tell your partner in a heartfelt way that you'd like to try something new to enhance your relationship. Emphasize how important this is to you.

We've found that even reluctant partners usually step up to the plate—and most want to continue even after the Surprise Date Challenge has ended.

One of our most cherished testimonials speaks directly to this situation:

Dear Dana & Marty,

I figured Justin wouldn't really want to participate in the Surprise Date Challenge, as I already plan dates to surprise him regularly. But he did, and I was shocked!

I thought our bond was pretty tight, but the Surprise Date Challenge has brought us closer. I relearned things about my husband that I had forgotten, and I've come to have a deeper love for him.

I've also learned to plan things around what he enjoys instead of always falling back on what I like to do. I took him to an indoor shooting range once—guns are not my favorite thing—and that really surprised him. He said he loved that I not only took him there, but participated. Then we played a few military games back at the house that I set up for him.

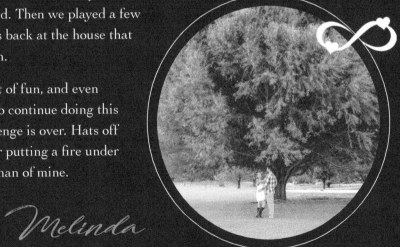

We've had a lot of fun, and even Justin wants to continue doing this after the challenge is over. Hats off to you both for putting a fire under this amazing man of mine.

Melinda

> **"** Do what you did in the beginning of a relationship and there won't be an end. **"**
>
> —Tony Robbins

Dana and I had our first surprise date—an Italian cooking class— a month into our relationship, on May 15, 2015, at Sur La Table in Scottsdale, Arizona.

Dana had no idea where we were going. I only told her to wear something cute, and to swap her usual high heels for comfortable shoes. When I picked her up, she looked radiant, and I could sense her excitement.

We held hands as the instructor described the pasta dish we'd be preparing, and we stole glances while chopping basil and dicing onions. We had a great time working side by side, making a meal that looked awesome and tasted amazing.

Knowing that Dana had as much fun as I did made me feel like a school kid again. We left the class ecstatic that we'd created something meaningful out of separate ingredients— the perfect analogy for our burgeoning relationship.

Marty

" Love is a vessel that
contains both security
and adventure, and
commitment offers
one of the great luxuries of life:
time. Marriage is not the end of
romance, it is the beginning. "

—Esther Perel

One of the best surprise dates I've ever planned for Marty was a weekend getaway. It was August and we needed to get out of the Phoenix heat, so we hopped in the car at noon on a Friday—with Marty at the wheel—and headed to Northern Arizona.

It was fun to keep Marty guessing when we passed an exit. Would it be the next one? Or the next? After about two hours, we arrived at our first destination, an extreme adventure course in Flagstaff. This was way outside my comfort zone, but I knew Marty would love it. As we slipped into harnesses for the zipline, the look on Marty's face was priceless—a win for both of us.

On our way to an Airbnb for the night, we made a pit stop at a winery for a tasting and delicious charcuterie plate. We reminisced about the adventure course and Marty tried to guess where we were going next… one of our favorite pizza bars.

The next morning, on our way home, we made a detour to the historic town of Jerome, where we toured local sites to learn more about the former mining community. We had wine with lunch and shopped at one of our favorite stores, Nellie Bly Kaleidoscopes—the largest dealer of kaleidoscopes in the world.

Marty's scorecard for the weekend: 10 out of 10.

Dana

Twelve Months of *Surprise* Dates

While the Surprise Date Challenge lasts only three months, we're confident you'll want to continue the fun, so here's a year's worth of date ideas. Use them as written, or put your own spin on them. Either way, we can personally vouch for every one—we've done them all!

The best part: Each date idea can be completed without dropping a lot of dough.

BIG NEW BEGINNINGS

LIFE IS FULL OF
Beautiful Moments
LET THEM IN

FUN FANTASY RITUAL
FFR
Creating Extraordinary Experiences

TODAY I AM... LOVE

EXPLORE

Road to Happines

Artistic Expression = Sensory Passion

2017

Body+Soul
SENSORY ESCAPES / WORDS: ANNA HART

| TASTE | SIGHT | SOUND | TOUCH | SMELL |

CELEBRATE EVERY

what's your passion?

I Am Here To Give And Receive Love!

A RICH LIFE IS ONE THAT ENRICHES OTHERS.

The place where dreams become reality

Getting Connected

Family and Friends

Santa Fe

JUST THE RIGHT AMOUNT *of* WRONG

LIVE YOUR BEST LIFE

Spheres of influen

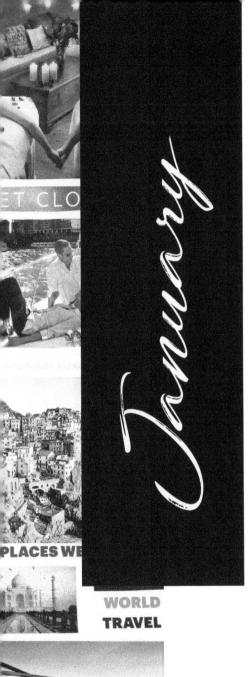

1

VISION BOARD

There's something about the first month of the year that conjures up infinite possibilities for what lies ahead.

Want to help manifest your dreams and desires? Create a vision board—a collage of images, words, and pictures that uses the law of attraction to bring what you want into the concrete world.

There is no right or wrong way to create one. You just want to feel happy and inspired when you look at it.

GATHER MATERIALS

1. Select a canvas for your creation.
   We like poster board or foam board.

2. Browse magazines for images and
   words that represent what you want
   to manifest in your life. Can't find
   anything that speaks to you?
   Print something from the web, or
   make your own.

3. Gather a few personal pictures.

GET TO WORK

1. Arrange images, words, and pictures
   on the board to get your desired look.

2. Glue each one to the board.

3. Display the board where you will see it
   every day.

4. Watch your dreams come true!

Cheri &
Vanessa

Together 5 years,
married 3 years,
3 kids.

"The Surprise Date Challenge *has provided a creative and fun date list for my wife and me to add to our crazy, hectic lives. The element of surprise is so exciting and fun.*" —Cheri

February

2

SCAVENGER HUNT

This one can be put together easily at the last minute.

Customize any of the clues we used for our surprise date—detailed on the next page—to fit your own relationship.

CLUE #1	… was a text message from Dana to Marty, alerting him to a scavenger hunt with a surprise ending: *"You are excellent at selecting this delicious beverage."*
CLUE #2	… was hidden in the wine fridge: *"Thinking about you really lights me up."*
CLUE #3	… was hidden in a lamp: *"I feel extra sexy when I'm wearing this."*
CLUE #4	… was hidden in a lingerie drawer: *"You look sexy when you're dancing."*
CLUE #5	… was hidden behind a photo of us dancing: *"Wow, our first kiss in my garage."*

That last clue led to a pillow on our bed, printed with a picture of us after our first kiss. With the pillow was a handwritten note of appreciation, along with a gift card to a favorite restaurant.

TIPS TO SIMPLIFY

Start with the end in mind. Where do you want your partner to wind up? Is a night out together the reward—or are you?

Once you know those answers, you're ready to create your clues. It's easiest to write them in reverse order. Be careful to make the clues easy enough to figure out, or the hunt will be more frustrating than fun.

How to come up with clues:

♥ Spend a few minutes thinking about some of the highlights of your relationship.

♥ What meaningful items or locations are relevant to some of those favorite relationship memories?

A TWIST

Have your partner find the clues at home while you wait at a restaurant. One clue may be a hint about what to wear; another might include instructions for picking up flowers along the way. Consider pre-ordering an Uber so your partner doesn't have to drive.

March

3

ROMANTIC TENT

Sometimes it's fun to act like a kid again and do silly things.

If you don't have the items listed here, they're easy enough to find online or at your local dollar store:

- ♥ Sheet or plastic tablecloth (the lighter the weight, the better)
- ♥ Clothespins
- ♥ White twinkly lights
- ♥ Battery-operated candles
- ♥ String or wire
- ♥ Two damage-free hanging hooks

Affix hooks on opposite walls in the bedroom, and connect with the string or wire. Wrap lights around the string, then drape a sheet on top. Clothespins attached to pillows on the bed add stability.

OTHER OPTIONS

Use a plastic tablecloth, which is lighter than a sheet and may stay up longer. Or go to a fabric store for super-lightweight tulle, or netting.

If you want to be less elaborate, you can always create a tent on the ground with a few sheets, chairs and/or other furniture.

Happy Tenting!

Christina &
Sergio

Together 6 years,
newly engaged.

"The Surprise Date Challenge helped get my fiancé and me out of the 'boring' dating rut.
We are always on the lookout for new ideas now. Best of all, I don't have to nag my fiancé anymore
to plan something." —Christina

April

4

ART NIGHT

Neither one of us has ever felt really artistic—probably because we tend to compare our work to others, which is never a good idea. We're all unique, so we should embrace our individuality and get creative!

For a paint night at home, turn to Pinterest for inspiration, then head to your local art supply store or browse the Internet for these supplies:

- ♥ Plastic tablecloth (to protect your floor)
- ♥ Easel
- ♥ Paint
- ♥ Paint brushes
- ♥ Canvas
- ♥ Palette or paper plate for paints

Lots of cities offer spots for group painting classes if you'd prefer a night out. Some classes have wine available, while others are BYOB. Check out Groupon to find specials in your area.

Not into painting? Search online for additional artistic ideas, such as glass blowing, drawing, and photography.

You both **deserve** to enjoy creating *your own* masterpiece. The sky's **the limit!**

Katie & Matt

Together 6 years,
married 5 years,
1 son.

"*Planning the surprise date for Matt was really fun and different than our normal routine of talking about work and our son. Our dinner date at the Dessert Botanical Gardens provided the perfect combination of exploration, with romance inside nooks and crannies along the way for stealing quick kisses. We are now Surprise Date'ers!*" —Katie

"*In our busy lives, surprise and spontaneity has been scarce and date night had become repetitive. Out of the blue, Katie said to be ready on Saturday for a surprise date. It was super cool to hear that, and I was excited and had a young-love feeling. Our adventure date and dinner was perfect, and I can't wait to plan a surprise date for her!*" —Matt

47

5

SPA DAY

There are so many ways to relax with a spa day.

The easiest and most luxurious way, of course, if your budget allows, is to book an experience at a beautiful resort. Schedule an early afternoon couples massage, facial, or body scrub—or do it all. Arrive early enough for lunch, relax at the pool, or use the other spa facilities before your treatment begins. Take a change of clothes to end your time at the resort with dinner and cocktails, or turn your experience into a staycation.

Why not try to score a deal? Look at midweek prices, which are usually cheaper than on weekends, and don't forget to check whether the resort is offering any specials on Groupon.

Or pamper yourselves with a manicure or pedicure at an upscale nail salon. Some even provide a glass of wine or champagne to get the party started.

A spa day in your own bathroom can also be fun. Take a romantic bubble bath with candles and champagne. (One of our favorite stores is Lush, which makes handmade bath products that are good for both you and the environment.)

Then take turns giving facials on the bed or couch. Here's what you'll need:

- ♥ Cleanser
- ♥ Exfoliant
- ♥ Mask
- ♥ Moisturizer
- ♥ Small bowl with warm water
- ♥ Washcloths
- ♥ Towels

Ambience is key here. Set the mood with low lighting, lots of candles, and calming music (we like Enya).

After cleaning your partner's face, gently use the exfoliant, then apply the mask. While the mask is doing its thing—it usually needs about 10 minutes—take advantage of the downtime to massage hands and feet. When ready, wipe off the mask with a washcloth—the towels protect sheets or couch cushions from getting wet—and finish with a full-body massage.

We are not responsible for what happens next...

6

June

MINI ROAD TRIP

Is there a place within two hours of where you live that you've both wanted to explore, but never have? If so, now's the time!

Do some advance research on your destination. The Internet and your chosen location's Chamber of Commerce are great resources for learning about the local scene.

Next, sketch out a timeline. Tell your partner when you'd like to leave for your excursion, as well as what to wear or pack.

Here's a sample itinerary for a morning departure:

STEP 1	Pack a delicious and hearty breakfast for the road, or stop at a diner along the way.
STEP 2	Once at your destination, go for a hike or bike ride—anything active.
STEP 3	Eat somewhere with a view or inviting patio—and good food, of course. Or dig into a pre-packed picnic lunch filled with your partner's favorite things to eat and drink.
STEP 4	Go shopping or explore the sights. Are there local landmarks to discover?
STEP 5	Be sure to take lots of pictures along the way!

Head back home with plenty of time to freshen up, so you can review the day's journey through stories and photos over dinner together.

Melinda & Justin

Known each other
35 years, married
16 years, 6 kids,
6 grandkids.

"I'm what you would call 'old-fashioned,' and by that I mean I may surprise my wife with flowers once every two or three years. Sad, I know. Dinner and a movie, then maybe drinks afterward, was my idea of a 'night out.' As men, we've been surprising our spouses with flowers and carcasses since we were hunter-gatherers. Some of us lack the romantic gene—myself included. Since becoming members of the Surprise Date community, my wife and I have created a union that has never been stronger. I love her more and more every day! We have been married 17 years and cannot wait to see what 17 more brings…Thank you." —Justin

July

7

SALSA DANCING

Dancing is by far one of the most romantic things a couple can do together—even if one person has two left feet.

Why not give salsa dancing a shot? It's known for being sensual and sexy.

Most communities have plenty of dance class options, so it shouldn't be too difficult to find a local studio for private or group lessons. Many include dance parties that allow students to practice new moves between classes.

Surprise your partner with a combination of private and group lessons.

After the first class—maybe make this one private for a more intimate introduction—head to a Spanish restaurant for tapas (small Spanish dishes) and a glass of red or white wine sangria.

Want a
Spanish-themed
night **without**
leaving the house?

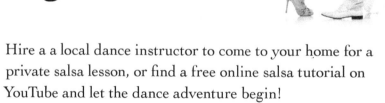

Hire a a local dance instructor to come to your home for a private salsa lesson, or find a free online salsa tutorial on YouTube and let the dance adventure begin!

Sheri & Brad

Friends 20 years,
committed 5 years,
6 kids.

"What started out as an obligation—otherwise known as 'my girlfriend's idea'—has built a deeper trust, even more love, a great deal of laughter, and a better bond to an already fantastic relationship." —Brad

"We have never laughed so hard. The Surprise Date Challenge *has been a game-changer in our relationship. This is such a simple concept, and the benefits are life-changing. The element of surprise will never get old!"* —Sheri

August

8

DIY PROJECT

Head to a thrift store to find a wooden piece of furniture, then stop by your local hardware store to pick up:

- ♥ Chalk paint
- ♥ Brushes
- ♥ Wax

What we love most about this DIY project is that it's simple, inexpensive, and you can create something for your home together.

1. Clean the furniture with a damp cloth.

2. Apply one or two coats of chalk paint.

3. Let dry completely. (Wait at least two hours.)

4. Optional: If you want a distressed look, use fine-grit sandpaper on a few areas.

5. Apply wax with a wax brush if you have one. A regular paint brush or rag will also get the job done.

6. Let dry for 24 hours.

Enjoy your
work *of* art!

Shiloh &
John

Together 8 years,
married 4 years,
2 kids.

"I know we're not having enough fun in our relationship when I feel disconnected from John. That's when it's the perfect time to plan a surprise date, as having more fun works wonders for any relationship." —Shiloh

"The Surprise Date Challenge helped us spice things up by increasing the passion and desire. We never knew what was going to unfold on our date." —John

9

COOKING CLASS

Cooking together is a great way to bond—and you'll be honing your culinary skills while spicing things up in the kitchen.

Look for a local cooking class, or consider hiring a chef to provide a private lesson in your home. Restaurants and hotels sometimes offer special-event cooking classes—from learning the proper way to hold a knife, to creating a culturally themed dish using the finest seasonal ingredients.

Want to keep things *simple* at home?

Before the date, buy a gorgeous cookbook, pick a few recipes to try, and buy the ingredients.

Wrap the cookbook to give as a gift when the date begins.

As an alternative, what about a lobster dinner delivered to your door? Several companies will ship to you directly.

Don't forget the dim lights, candles, and background music. Maybe some Michael Bublé or Frank Sinatra?

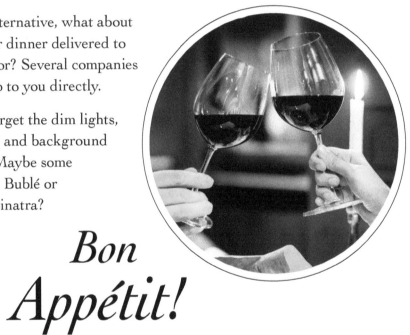

Bon Appétit!

10 VOLUNTEERING

Giving back to your community is an important way to connect with others and each other. For us, it's a priceless reminder that we are blessed beyond measure.

Many people wait until the holidays to volunteer, but local charities are always looking—and extremely grateful—for assistance.

Here are some places where you can make a difference:

- ♥ Homeless shelter
- ♥ Food bank
- ♥ Habitat for Humanity
- ♥ Animal shelter
- ♥ Senior center
- ♥ Festival or other local event

November

11

TROPICAL ISLAND

When the weather starts to cool down, why not plan a faux trip to the tropics indoors? Turn up the heat on your thermostat and throw on your favorite swimsuit or summer clothes.

Pack a beach bag with anything you would enjoy on a hot summer day—minus the suntan lotion!

Bonus: If you have lounge chairs, bring them inside and pretend you're at the pool, beach, or Bahamas. Make some cold cocktails or non-alcoholic mocktails.

Relaxation is the name of the game, so grab a book you've wanted to read or that stack of magazines you may have growing ever taller in the corner. Have some of your go-to summer snacks ready, and don't forget the ice cream or popsicles.

Skinny-dipping in the bathtub is optional!

December

12 GINGERBREAD HOUSE

All those yummy graham crackers, gumdrops, candy canes…

Who says decorating a gingerbread house is just for kids?

December 8th is Gingerbread Decorating Day, and December 12th is Gingerbread House Day—perfect reasons to make your own delectable dwelling.

OPTION 1

Search the Internet for gingerbread house decorating events in your area. We've found both free and paid events that provide supplies to build your very own masterpiece.

OPTION 2

Shop online or at a store for a gingerbread house kit to create in the comfort of your own home. To spark curiosity without giving away too many details, consider wrapping holiday or gingerbread-themed PJs—or a onesie—as a gift with the surprise date invitation. Then get to work in your holiday garb while sipping hot chocolate, apple cider, or your favorite holiday beverage.

Have a fireplace? Cuddle up afterward in front of the flames to turn up the heat.

Marie & Derek

High school sweethearts, together over 16 years, 3 kids.

"We fell into the trap of putting our children first and placing date nights on the back burner due to tight budgets. The Surprise Date Challenge and the 'Free Date' ideas allowed me to show my partner renewed and thoughtful effort, which is a huge plus for our family of five." —Marie

"I loved being surprised by Marie, and felt deeply appreciated and reminded how much I'm loved. I'm definitely sharing the Surprise Date Challenge with my friends!" —Derek

"Do not spoil what you have by desiring what you have not; remember that what you now have was once among the things you only hoped for."

—Epicurus

Being the Happiest Couple You Know

Like most of us, you've probably had your fair share of trial-and-error moments while trying to create a healthy, loving relationship. Too bad there's no magic wand to wave, guaranteeing that simply saying "I love you" would support and sustain a long-term partnership. Certainly those words are vitally important, but they aren't enough.

While it's true that a successful relationship takes work, we've swapped "work" with some ABCs.

AFFINITY	The harmonious connection we forge with our partner. As Aristotle once said, together we can create a stronger whole.
BALANCE	The necessary ingredient that forges individuality within a couple, and helps with achieving compromise.
COMMUNICATION	The central core of a respectful, trusting relationship. Without effective conversations, affinity and balance retreat and get replaced with complacency.

We may not have a magic wand, but we do know—from our experience and the experiences of our clients—that planning just one monthly surprise date for each other can make you the happiest couple you know.

And, well, that's **Magic** in *our* **book.**

"After being married 32 years, it's easy to get stuck in
a rut of doing the same things. We've rekindled the
romance and passion we had at the beginning
of our relationship."

Mark &
Betty

"After 27 years of marriage and raising two amazing
children while building successful businesses,
we've seen firsthand how daily routines left us feeling
disconnected at times. Planning 'outside the box' dates
has significantly reinvigorated our relationship."

Kelly
& Rusty

79

The Surprise Date Inspiration Kit
is where you can put your
ABCs to work immediately!

Simply visit
www.SurpriseDateChallenge.com
and download your own Inspiration Kit
including instructions, the Surprise Date
Proclamation, and additional date ideas to
get your Surprise Date Challenge underway.

LET'S GET THIS PARTY STARTED!

LET IT BE KNOWN...

That on _____ a Proclamation for the
Surprise Date between _____ and _____ has been
officially Declared and Agreed upon. _____ and _____ met
in person for the first time on _____ at _____ in
_____ and agree that in celebration of their relationship and in keeping said
partnership exceptional, exciting and fun, do hereby declare and establish their *Surprise Date.*

THE PARTIES unequivocally agree to alternate responsibility for planning each month's
Surprise Date that shall commence on the Proclamation date above. The Surprise Date planner
shall communicate said Surprise Date plans to the other party no later than four (4) hours
prior to actual Surprise Date and those that follow until terminated by both Parties in writing.
Bottom-line... no procrastinating and late fees apply!

THE PARTIES agree that all Surprise Date activities and events must consist of and include
at least three (3) of the following events/activities/experiences: Fun, Excitement, Invigorating,
A "first" for both, Adventure, Travel, Staycation, Athleticism, Artistic, Creativity, Mystery, Intrigue,
Laughter, Sexuality, Sensuality, Mind-blowing, Passion, Educational, or other activities or
events mutually agreed upon by the Parties.

We think we've covered or uncovered things you can do that are fun in either a vertical or
horizontal position!

The authorized signatures of both Parties show consent to this Agreement which shall be
executed and sealed with a passionate kiss.

NAME	**NAME**
SIGNATURE	**SIGNATURE**

Download your own Proclamation by joining the
"Surprise Date Club" on our website, SurpriseDateChallenge.com.

CPSIA information can be obtained
at www.ICGtesting.com
Printed in the USA
LVHW070727170620
658107LV00007B/336

9 781733 720809